Notable Quotables

Compiled by Jerry Reedy

Copyright © 1986 by
World Book, Inc., *formerly* the
World Book-Childcraft
International, Inc.
Chicago, Illinois 60654

All rights reserved. This volume may not be
reproduced in whole or in part in any form without
written permission from the publishers.

Printed in the United States of America

published by
World Book Encyclopedia, Inc.
a Scott Fetzer company
Chicago

Printed in the United States of America

ISBN 0-7166-3172-5
Library of Congress Catalog Card No. 84-51513
a/hd

Contents

Quotations

Whether you need to find an old, familiar saying or simply wish to find a fresh, new way of expressing an idea, *Notable Quotables* can help you do it. The quotations are organized into more than 100 different subject categories; the subjects are arranged in alphabetical order. Within each category, the quotations appear in chronological order, beginning with proverbs and the ideas of ancient thinkers, and ending with comments by people in our own time.

When you need a quotation on a given subject, you might have to look under several different headings in order to find just the right one. If, for example, you were looking for quotations about heroes, you could also look under *Ability, Bravery, Character, Courage, Strength, Success,* and *Valor.*

Even if you find no quotations that seem just right, you're apt to find one or more that will help to clarify or stimulate your thinking on a subject. Here are a pair of stimulating quotes on the subject of beauty. As in many other subject areas, you'll find a wide divergence of opinion and point of view. First the immortal words of John Keats:

> "A thing of beauty is a joy forever:
> Its loveliness increases; it will never
> Pass into nothingness."

Contrast these noble thoughts with those of Voltaire on the same subject:

> "Ask a toad what is beauty . . .; he will answer that it is a female with two great round eyes, coming out of her little head, a large, flat mouth, a yellow belly and a brown back."

This wide variety of material within each subject category should help you find quotations that are appropriate for the point you are trying to make.

Tips for Using Quotations

The following are some tips for using quotations properly in your writing and speaking:

Tip number one: Don't assume that peppering your writing or speaking with famous quotations will automatically assure its success. If you overdo it, the opposite will happen. It's one thing to use quotations to illuminate and substantiate what you're speaking or writing about, but it's quite another to make them carry the whole burden. If two-thirds of what you have to say on a subject is simply parroted, your listeners or readers will begin to grumble.

Tip number two: Make every quotation count. Don't put one in just because it has a nice ring to it or has something remotely to do with your subject. If it doesn't make your point better than you could have made it yourself, leave it out.

Tip number three: Don't be afraid to edit. If there's any part of a quote that doesn't add something relevant, cut it out. A case in point is something Harry Truman once said about statesmen:

> "A politician is a man who understands government, and it takes a politician to run a govern-

ment. A statesman is a politician who's been dead 10 or 15 years."

The first sentence, meritorious and useful as it may have been in some other context, doesn't mention anything about statesmen. Though it leads into the second sentence, the second sentence stands alone quite successfully—and packs more punch by itself. If you want to quote Harry Truman on statesmen or statesmanship, you're better off leaving the first sentence out.

Tip number four: It's not only the quote itself that matters, but the person who utters it. Hence, if you're substantiating a thought about World War II, you might want to cite Winston Churchill, since he is universally recognized as an authority on the subject. If you want to quote a valid opinion about the movies, pick somebody like Katharine Hepburn or Ingmar Bergman.

Tip number five: Use common sense and good taste when selecting quotations. Elisabeth Kubler-Ross has written wisely and eloquently on the subject of death and has undoubtedly helped millions of people come to terms with the loss of a loved one. In one of her books, she wrote of death, in part:

> ". . .the only thing you lose is something you don't need anymore. . .your physical body. It's like putting away your winter coat when spring comes."

These words would no doubt console someone reading the book, but taken by themselves, they would hardly be appropriate if spoken to a group of people who had just learned that they were terminally ill. Taste, good judgment, sensitivity—all are extremely important when adopting the words of others—especially under trying circumstances.

Finally, just this reminder: the ability to use quotations effectively can do much more than simply enhance your reading and writing. Properly used, quotations can have the power to change the humdrum into the exciting, the merely good into the truly great. And all the best people do it. But don't take our word for it; read the words of Michel de Montaigne:

> "I quote the others only to better express myself."

W. I. E. Gates put it even more emphatically:

> "Stronger than an army is a quotation whose time has come."

Ability

Behind an able man there are always other able men.
Chinese proverb

Everyone must row with the oars he has.
English proverb

The winds and waves are always on the side of the ablest navigators.
Edward Gibbon

A man must not deny his manifest abilities, for that is to evade his obligations.
Robert Louis Stevenson

Adversity

In the day of prosperity be joyful, but in the day of adversity consider.
> *Ecclesiastes 7:14*

Fire is the test of gold; adversity, of strong men.
> *Lucius Annaeus Seneca*

In every kind of adversity, the bitterest part of a man's affliction is to remember that he once was happy.
> *Manilus Severinus Boethius*

Prosperity getteth friends, but adversity trieth them.
> *Nicholas Ling*

Adversity makes a man wise, not rich.
> *John Ray*

Adversity is the state in which a man most easily becomes acquainted with himself, being especially free from admirers then.
> *Samuel Johnson*

By trying, we can easily learn to endure adversity. Another man's, I mean.
> *Mark Twain*

When you are down and out, something always turns up—and it is usually the noses of your friends.
> *Orson Welles*

Advice

Advice is like kissing: it costs nothing and is a pleasant thing to do.
> *George Bernard Shaw*

Ambition

What shall it profit a man, if he shall gain the whole world, and lose his own soul?
> *Mark 8:36*

Ambition drove many men to become false; to have one thought locked in the breast, another ready on the tongue.
> *Sallust*

A man's worth is no greater than the worth of his ambitions.
> *Marcus Aurelius*

Nothing arouses ambition so much in the heart as the trumpet-clang of another's fame.
> *Baltasar Gracián*

Ambition is the last refuge of the failure.
> *Oscar Wilde*

Keep away from people who try to belittle your ambitions. Small people always do that, but the really great make you feel that you, too, can become great.
> *Mark Twain*

Don't be afraid to take a big step. You can't cross a chasm in two small jumps.
> *David Lloyd George*

Ambition and suspicion always go together.
> *Georg Christoph Lichtenberg*

All sins have their origin in a sense of inferiority, otherwise called ambition.
> *Cesare Pavese*

He who does not hope to win has already lost.
José Joaquín Olmedo

An ambitious man can never know peace.
J. Krishnamurti

He who would leap high must take a long run.
Danish proverb

Anger

Let not the sun go down upon your wrath.
Ephesians 4:26

He that is slow to anger is better than the mighty:
and he that ruleth his spirit than he that taketh a city.
Proverbs 16:32

I was angry with my foe: I told it not, my wrath did
grow.
William Blake

Anger is never without a reason, but seldom with a
good one.
Benjamin Franklin

When angry, count ten before you speak; if very
angry, a hundred.
Thomas Jefferson

Nothing on earth consumes a man more quickly
than the passion of resentment.
Friedrich Nietzsche

The world needs anger. The world often continues to
allow evil because it isn't angry enough.
Bede Jarrett

Apathy

Shame on the soul, to falter on the road of life while the body still perseveres.

Marcus Aurelius

Nothing is more conducive to peace of mind than not having any opinion at all.

Georg Christoph Lichtenberg

Most of us have no real loves and no real hatreds. Blessed is love, less blessed is hatred, but thrice accursed is that indifference which is neither one nor the other.

Mark Rutherford

By far the most dangerous foe we have to fight is apathy—indifference from whatever cause, not from a lack of knowledge, but from carelessness, from absorption in other pursuits, from a contempt bred of self-satisfaction.

Sir William Osler

It's extraordinary how we go through life with eyes half shut, with dull ears, with dormant thoughts. Perhaps it's just as well; and it may be that it is this very dullness that makes life to the incalculable majority so supportable and so welcome.

Joseph Conrad

Science may have found a cure for most evils; but it has found no remedy for the worst of them all—the apathy of human beings.

Helen Keller

Emotion is the chief source of all becoming-conscious. There can be no transforming of darkness into light and of apathy into movement without emotion.

Carl Gustav Jung

The death of democracy is not likely to be an assassination from ambush. It will be a slow extinction from apathy, indifference, and undernourishment.

Robert Maynard Hutchins

By appreciation, we make excellence in others our own property.

Voltaire

Art

Art is simply a right method of doing things. The test of the artist does not lie in the will with which he goes to work, but in the excellence of the work he produces.

Saint Thomas Aquinas

Nature seldom gives us the very best; for that we must have recourse to art.

Baltasar Gracián

We must never forget that art is not a form of propaganda; it is a form of truth.

John Fitzgerald Kennedy

The aim of every artist is to arrest motion, which is life, by artificial means and hold it fixed so that a hundred years later, when a stranger looks at it, it moves again since it is life.

William Faulkner

If your work of art is good, if it is true, it will find its echo and make its place—in six months, in six years, or after you are gone. What is the difference?
  Gustave Flaubert

Without art, the crudeness of reality would make the world unbearable.
  George Bernard Shaw

The artist is only given to sense more keenly than others the harmony of the world and all the beauty and savagery of the human contribution to it—and to communicate this poignantly to people.
  Alexander Solzhenitsyn

Authority

The man whose authority is recent is always stern.
  Aeschylus

Authority without wisdom is like a heavy ax without an edge, fitter to bruise than polish.
  Anne Bradstreet

Lawful and settled authority is very seldom resisted when it is well employed.
  Samuel Johnson

There are two ways of establishing a proposition. One is by trying to demonstrate it upon reason; and the other is, to show that great men in former times have thought so and so, and thus to pass it on by pure authority.
  Abraham Lincoln

Every great advance in natural knowledge has involved the absolute rejection of authority.
  Thomas Henry Huxley

When you are saying something which doesn't mean much, you must say it with a great deal of authority.
  Virgil Thomson

Authority has every reason to fear the skeptic, for authority can rarely survive in the face of doubt.
  Robert Lindner

You can delegate authority, but you can never delegate responsibility for delegating a task to someone else. If you picked the right man, fine, but if you picked the wrong man, the responsibility is yours—not his.
  Richard E. Krafve

Beauty

Everything has its beauty, but not everyone sees it.
  Confucius

It is a beautiful bird which gets caged.
  Chinese proverb

All the orators are dumb where beauty pleadeth.
  William Shakespeare

Whenever, at a party, I have been in the mood to study fools, I have always looked for a great beauty; they always gather round her like flies around a fruit-stall.
  Johann Paul Friedrich Richter

Beauty is truth, truth beauty,—that is all ye know on earth, and all ye need to know.

John Keats

Beauty is its own excuse for being.

Ralph Waldo Emerson

Remember that the most beautiful things in the world are the most useless: peacocks and lilies, for instance.

John Ruskin

Beauty is in the eye of the beholder.

Margaret Wolfe Hungerford

Belief

All things are possible to one who believes.

Saint Bernard of Clairvaux

To believe with certainty we must begin with doubting.

Stanislas I, King of Poland

Believe only half of what you see and nothing that you hear.

Dinah Mulock Craik

All ages of belief have been great; all of unbelief have been mean.

Ralph Waldo Emerson

Believe that life is worth living, and your belief will help create the fact.

William James

He who is swift to believe is swift to forget.
> *Abraham Joshua Heschel*

Bravery

It is easy to be brave from a safe distance.
> *Aesop*

Fortune favors the brave.
> *Terence*

None but the brave deserves the fair.
> *John Dryden*

Some have been thought brave because they were afraid to run away.
> *Thomas Fuller*

Bravery never goes out of fashion.
> *William Makepeace Thackeray*

Bravery is the capacity to perform properly even when scared half to death.
> *Gen. Omar Nelson Bradley*

Business

Few people do business well who do nothing else.
> *Lord Chesterfield*

Corporation: An ingenious device for obtaining individual profit without individual responsibility.
> *Ambrose Bierce*

Business underlies everything in our national life, including our spiritual life. Witness the fact that in the Lord's Prayer, the first petition is for daily bread. No one can worship God or love his neighbor on an empty stomach.

Woodrow Wilson

The business of America is business.

Calvin Coolidge

A conference is just an admission that you want somebody to join you in your troubles.

Will Rogers

Career

Blessed is he who has found his work; let him ask no other blessedness.

Thomas Carlyle

Every calling is great when greatly pursued.

Oliver Wendell Holmes, Jr.

The vocation of every man and woman is to serve other people.

Leo Tolstoy

The test of a vocation is the love of the drudgery it involves.

Logan Pearsall Smith

Whenever it is in any way possible, every boy and girl should choose as his life work some occupation which he should like to do anyhow, even if he did not need the money.

William Lyon Phelps

The price one pays for pursuing any profession, or calling, is an intimate knowledge of its ugly side.
James Baldwin

Chance

Enjoy yourself, drink, call the life you live today your own, but only that, the rest belongs to chance.
Euripides

The race is not to the swift, nor the battle to the strong, neither yet bread to the wise, nor yet riches to men of understanding, nor yet favor to men of skill; but time and chance happeneth to them all.
Ecclesiastes 9:11

Although men flatter themselves with their great actions, they are not so often the result of a great design as of chance.
François de La Rochefoucauld

Success is a fickle jade. The clothes on her back may be put there by hard work, but her jewels are the gifts of chance.
Sir Charles Wheeler

A wise man turns chance into good fortune.
Thomas Fuller

I claim not to have controlled events, but confess plainly that events have controlled me.
Abe Lincoln

Every possession and every happiness is but lent by chance for an uncertain time, and may therefore be demanded back the next hours.
Arthur Schopenhauer

Change

Nothing is permanent but change.
Heraclitus

The absurd man is he who never changes.
Auguste Barthélémy

An individual is more apt to change, perhaps, than all the world around him.
Daniel Webster

To live is to change, and to be perfect is to have changed often.
Cardinal Newman

All changes, even the most longed for, have their melancholy; for what we leave behind us is a part of ourselves, we must die to one life before we can enter into another!
Anatole France

Great cultural changes begin in affectation and end in routine.
Jacques Barzun

To remain young one must change. The perpetual campus hero is not a young man but an old boy.
Alexander Chase

We live in a moment of history where change is so speeded up that we begin to see the present only when it is already disappearing.
R. D. Laing

Change is the law of life. And those who look only to the past or the present are certain to miss the future.
John Fitzgerald Kennedy

Character

A good character carries with it the highest power of causing a thing to be believed.
Aristotle

Character is much easier kept than recovered.
Thomas Paine

Character is like a tree and reputation like its shadow. The shadow is what we think of it; the tree is the real thing.
Abraham Lincoln

Character cannot be developed in ease and quiet. Only through experience of trial and suffering can the soul be strengthened, vision cleared, ambition inspired, and success achieved.
Helen Keller

Children

Use only nine parts of your shrewdness; reserve one part for the benefit of your children.
Chinese proverb

Trees are for shade, and children for old age.
Chinese proverb

My own daughters, whenever they shall grow to years of discretion, I am determined to throw into a great kettle and boil till they are clean.
John Adams

If you wish to study men you must not neglect to mix with the society of children.
Jesse Torrey

There never was a child so lovely but his mother was glad to get him asleep.
> Ralph Waldo Emerson

That energy which makes a child hard to manage is the energy which afterward makes him a manager in life.
> Henry Ward Beecher

Nature makes boys and girls lovely to look upon so they can be tolerated until they acquire some sense.
> William Lyon Phelps

Reasoning with a child is fine, if you can reach the child's reason without destroying your own.
> John Mason Brown

I have found the best way to give advice to your children is to find out what they want and then advise them to do it.
> Harry Truman

What's done to children, they will do to society.
> Karl Augustus Menninger

Once you've loved a child, you love all children. You give away your love to one, and you find that by the giving you have made yourself an inexhaustible treasury.
> Margaret Lee Runbeck, Our Miss Boo

Pretty much all the honest truthtelling there is in the world is done by children.
> Don Herold

Juvenile appraisals of other juveniles make up in clarity what they lack in charity.
>*Edgar Z. Friedenberg*

One of the most obvious facts about grownups to a child, is that they have forgotten what it is like to be a child.
>*Randall Jarrell*

Children have never been good at listening to their elders, but they have never failed to imitate them.
>*James Baldwin*

Your children need your presence more than your presents.
>*Jesse Jackson*

Civilization

A sufficient measure of civilization is the influence of good women.
>*Ralph Waldo Emerson*

Civilization degrades the many to exalt the few.
>*Bronson Alcott*

Civilization is the lamb's skin in which barbarism masquerades.
>*Thomas Bailey Aldrich*

An Englishman who was wrecked on a strange shore and wandering along the coast came to a gallows with a victim hanging on it, and fell down on his knees and thanked God that he at last beheld a sign of civilization.
>*James Garfield*

You can't say civilization won't advance, . . . for
in every war they kill you a new way.
    Will Rogers

Civilization is a movement and not a condition, a
voyage and not a harbor.
    Arnold Toynbee

Civilization begins with order, grows with liberty and
dies with chaos.
    Will Durant

Conformity

We should know mankind better if we were not so
anxious to resemble one another.
    Johann Wolfgang von Goethe

We are half ruined by conformity, but we should be
wholly ruined without it.
    Charles Dudley Warner

There is truth in the high opinion that in so far as a
man conforms, he ceases to exist.
    Max Eastman

In almost any society, I think, the quality of the non-
conformists is likely to be just as good as and no
better than that of the conformists.
    Margaret Mead

Success, recognition, and conformity are the by-
words of the modern world where everyone seems to
crave the anesthetizing security of being identified
with the majority.
    Martin Luther King, Jr.

Conscience

A guilty conscience needs no accuser.
English proverb

The glory of good men is in their conscience and not in the mouths of men.
Thomas à Kempis

Conscience is, in most men, an anticipation of the opinion of others.
Henry Taylor

Conscience is the name which the orthodox give to their prejudices.
John Oliver Hobbes

Our conscience is not the vessel of eternal verities. It grows with our social life, and a new social condition means a radical change in conscience.
Walter Lippmann

Conscience is the inner voice which warns us that someone may be looking.
H. L. Mencken

Your conscience is what your mother told you before you were six years old.
Dr. G. Brock Chisholm

Having a conscience does not prevent us from sinning; it merely prevents us from enjoying it.
Bits & Pieces

Courage

This is courage in a man: to bear unflinchingly what heaven sends.
Euripides

No one can answer for his courage when he has never been in danger.
> François de La Rochefoucauld

Keep your fears to yourself, but share your courage.
> Robert Louis Stevenson

Courage is resistance to fear, mastery of fear—not absence of fear. Except a creature be part coward it is not a compliment to say it is brave.
> Mark Twain

Courage is fear that has said its prayers.
> Karle Baker

Until the day of his death, no man can be sure of his courage.
> Jean Anouilh

Criticism

The blow of a whip raises a welt, but a blow of the tongue crushes bones.
> Apocrypha, Ecclesiasticus 28:17

They have a right to censure that have a heart to help.
> William Penn

If a man is often the subject of conversation he soon becomes the subject of criticism.
> Immanuel Kant

No man can tell another his faults so as to benefit him, unless he loves him.
> Henry Ward Beecher

To criticize is to neither praise or denounce, but to get nearer your subject.
John Butler Yeats

I have never found, in a long experience of politics, that criticism is ever inhibited by ignorance.
Harold Macmillan

A critic is a man who knows the way but can't drive the car.
Kenneth Tynan

Death

To die with glory, if one has to die at all, is still, I think, pain for the dier.
Euripides

Any man's death diminishes me, because I am involved in mankind; and therefore never send to know for whom the bell tolls; it tolls for thee.
John Donne

He who fears death dies every time he thinks of it.
Stanislas I, King of Poland

I am dying, as I have lived, beyond my means.
Oscar Wilde

Death is the supreme festival on the road to freedom.
Dietrich Bonhoeffer

If even dying is to be made a social function, then, please, grant me the favor of sneaking out on tiptoe without disturbing the party.
Dag Hammarskjöld

I've come to look upon death the same way I look upon root-canal work. Everyone else seems to get through it all right, so it couldn't be too difficult for me.

Joseph Heller

It's a blessing to die for a cause, because you can so easily die for nothing.

Andrew Young

Defense

A man without a stick will be bitten even by sheep.

Hindu proverb

To be prepared for war is one of the most effectual means of preserving peace.

George Washington

Be as beneficent as the sun or the sea, but if your rights as a rational being are trenched on, die on the first inch of your territory.

Ralph Waldo Emerson

No nation ever had an army large enough to guarantee it against attack in time of peace or insure it victory in time of war.

Calvin Coolidge

The core of our defense is the faith we have in the institutions we defend.

Franklin Delano Roosevelt

It is an unfortunate fact that we can secure peace only by preparing for war.

John Fitzgerald Kennedy

Democracy

Democracy arose from men thinking that if they are equal in any respect they are equal in all respects.
Aristotle

If liberty and equality, as is thought by some, are chiefly to be found in democracy, they will be best attained when all persons alike share in the government to the utmost.
Aristotle

Every government degenerates when trusted to the rulers of the people alone. The people themselves therefore are its only safe depositories.
Thomas Jefferson

No man is good enough to govern another man without that other's consent.
Abraham Lincoln

I believe in democracy because it releases the energies of every human being.
Woodrow Wilson

It would be folly to argue that the people cannot make political mistakes. They can and do make grave mistakes. They know it, they pay the penalty, but compared with the mistakes which have been made by every kind of autocracy they are unimportant.
Calvin Coolidge

All the ills of democracy can be cured by more democracy.
Alfred E. Smith

One of the evils of democracy is, you have to put up with the man you elect whether you want him or not.
> *Will Rogers*

Democracy means government by discussion but it is only effective if you can stop people talking.
> *Clement Attlee*

Democracy is a small hard core of common agreement, surrounded by a rich variety of individual differences.
> *James B. Conant*

Desire

The desire for imaginary benefits often involves the loss of present blessings.
> *Aesop*

If you desire many things, many things will seem but a few.
> *Benjamin Franklin*

The fewer the desires, the more peace.
> *Thomas Wilson*

There are two tragedies in life. One is not to get your heart's desire. The other is to get it.
> *George Bernard Shaw*

Often, the thing we pursue most passionately is but a substitute for the one thing we really want and cannot have.
> *Eric Hoffer*

Despair

Despair exaggerates not only our misery but also our weakness.

> *Marquis de Vauvenargues*

The mass of men lead lives of quiet desperation. What is called resignation is confirmed desperation.

> *Henry David Thoreau*

What's the good being hopeless, so long as one has a hobnailed boot to kick with?

> *D. H. Lawrence*

Despair is the price one pays for setting oneself an impossible aim.

> *Graham Greene*

To eat bread without hope is still slowly to starve to death.

> *Pearl S. Buck*

We can destroy ourselves by cynicism and disillusion, just as effectively as by bombs.

> *Kenneth Clark*

Education

The direction in which education starts a man, will determine his future life.

> *Plato*

Men learn while they teach.

> *Seneca*

'Tis education forms the common mind;
Just as the twig is bent the tree's inclined.

> *Alexander Pope*

Education makes a people easy to lead but difficult to drive; easy to govern, but impossible to enslave.
   Lord Henry Peter Brougham

The man who reads nothing at all is better educated than the man who reads nothing but newspapers.
   Thomas Jefferson

In the first place God made idiots. This was for practice. Then He made School Boards.
   Mark Twain

I have never let my schooling interfere with my education.
   Mark Twain

What is really important in education is not that the child learns this and that, but that the mind is matured, that energy is aroused.
   Søren Kierkegaard

Education: That which discloses to the wise and disguises from the foolish their lack of understanding.
   Ambrose Bierce

The test and use of man's education is that he finds pleasure in the exercise of his mind.
   Jacques Barzun

Much education today is monumentally ineffective. All too often we are giving young people cut flowers when we should be teaching them to grow their own plants.
   John W. Gardner

Emotion

Seeing's believing, but feeling is God's own truth.
  Irish proverb

Trust not to thy feeling, for whatever it be now, it
will quickly be changed into another thing.
  Thomas à Kempis

Men, as well as women, are much oftener led by
their hearts than by their understandings.
  Lord Chesterfield

The advantage of the emotions is that they lead us
astray.
  Oscar Wilde

The important thing is being capable of emotions,
but to experience only one's own would be a sorry
limitation.
  André Gide

Cherish your emotions and never undervalue them.
  Robert Henri

In a full heart there is room for everything, and in an
empty heart there is room for nothing.
  Antonio Porchia

Equality

Before God and the bus driver we are all equal.
  German proverb

The only stable state is the one in which all men are
equal before the law.
  Aristotle

There is no merit in equality, unless it be equality with the best.
>   *John Lancaster Spalding*

The Lord so constituted everybody that no matter what color you are you require the same amount of nourishment.
>   *Will Rogers*

We clamor for equality chiefly in matters in which we ourselves cannot hope to obtain excellence.
>   *Eric Hoffer*

To live anywhere in the world today and be against equality because of race or color, is like living in Alaska and being against snow.
>   *William Faulkner*

Faith

Faith is to believe what you do not yet see; the reward for this faith is to see what you believe.
>   *Saint Augustine*

It is by believing in roses that one brings them to bloom.
>   *French proverb*

Despotism may govern without faith, but Liberty cannot.
>   *Alexis de Tocqueville*

Faith is like love: it cannot be forced.
>   *Arthur Schopenhauer*

All the scholastic scaffolding falls, as a ruined edifice, before one single word—faith.
>   *Napoleon*

Religious faith, indeed, relates to that which is above us, but it must arise from that which is within us.
Josiah Royce

Faith is believing what you know ain't so.
Mark Twain

It is faith and not reason which impels men to action . . . Intelligence is content to point out the road but never drives us along it.
Alexis Carrel

Fame

I was a man given to the vanities of the world, whose chief delight consisted in martial exercises, with a great and vain desire to win renown.
Saint Ignatius of Loyola

I was the toast of two continents: Greenland and Australia.
Dorothy Parker

Father

It is a wise father that knows his own child.
William Shakespeare

There must always be a struggle between a father and son, while one aims at power and the other at independence.
Samuel Johnson

I could not point to any need in childhood as strong as that for a father's protection.
Sigmund Freud

The fundamental defect of fathers is that they want their children to be a credit to them.
Bertrand Russell

You don't have to deserve your mother's love. You have to deserve your father's.
Robert Frost

Fault

If the best man's faults were written on his forehead, it would make him pull his hat over his eyes.
Gaelic proverb

We forget our faults easily when they are known to ourselves alone.
François de La Rochefoucauld

A benevolent man should allow a few faults in himself, to keep his friends in countenance.
Benjamin Franklin

The greatest of faults, I should say, is to be conscious of none.
Thomas Carlyle

People who have no faults are terrible; there is no way of taking advantage of them.
Anatole France

It is in our faults and failings, not in our virtues, that we touch one another and find sympathy.
Jerome K. Jerome

None of us can stand other people having the same faults as ourselves.
Oscar Wilde

Fear

Fear is stronger than arms.
Aeschylus

He who fears something gives it power over him.
Moorish proverb

No passion so effectually robs the mind of all its powers of acting and reasoning as fear.
Edmund Burke

The wise man in the storm prays God, not for safety from danger, but for deliverance from fear. It is the storm within which endangers him, not the storm without.
Ralph Waldo Emerson

A good scare is worth more to a man than good advice.
Edgar Watson Howe

The only thing we have to fear is fear itself—nameless, unreasoning, unjustified terror which paralyzes needed efforts to convert retreat into advance.
Franklin Delano Roosevelt

Freedom

Better starve free than be a fat slave.
Aesop

I believe each individual is naturally entitled to do as he pleases with himself and the fruits of his labor, so far as it in no way interferes with any other men's rights.
Abraham Lincoln

This is a world of compensations; and he who be no slave must consent to have no slave. Those who deny freedom to others deserve it not for themselves; and, under a just God, cannot long retain it.
    Abraham Lincoln

It is a worthy thing to fight for one's freedom; it is another sight finer to fight for another man's.
    Mark Twain

To know how to free oneself is nothing; the arduous thing is to know what to do with one's freedom.
    André Gide

It is better to die on your feet than to live on your knees.
    Dolores Ibarruri

"Freedom from Fear" could be said to sum up the whole philosophy of human rights.
    Dag Hammarskjöld

There can be no real freedom without the freedom to fail.
    Eric Hoffer

The basic test of freedom is perhaps less in what we are free to do than in what we are free not to do.
    Eric Hoffer

Friendship

Friendship is a single soul dwelling in two bodies.
    Aristotle

Forsake not an old friend, for a new one does not compare with him.
    Apocrypha, Ecclesiasticus 9:10

38

Without a good mirror no lady can know her true appearance; without a true friend no gentleman can know his own errors of conduct.
    Chinese proverb

Friendships renewed demand more care than those which have never been broken.
    François de La Rochefoucauld

The best way to wipe out a friendship is to sponge on it.
    S. J. Gudge

Tart words make no friends; a spoonful of honey will catch more flies than a gallon of vinegar.
    Benjamin Franklin

Friendship is like money, easier made than kept.
    Samuel Butler

The only way to have a friend is to be one.
    Ralph Waldo Emerson

A friend is one before whom I may think aloud.
    Ralph Waldo Emerson

The better part of one's life consists of his friend-ships.
    Abraham Lincoln

The loss of enemies does not compensate for the loss of friends.
    Abraham Lincoln

It is one of the blessings of old friends that you can afford to be stupid with them.
    Ralph Waldo Emerson

Friendship's the wine of life.
Edward Young

Every time I paint a portrait I lose a friend.
John Singer Sargent

One of the quickest ways to meet new people is to pick up the wrong ball on a golf course.
Bits & Pieces

Future

If a man takes no thought about what is distant, he will find sorrow near at hand.
Confucius

The future you shall know when it has become; before then, forget it.
Aeschylus

He that fears not the future may enjoy the present.
Thomas Fuller

I like the dreams of the future better than the history of the past.
Thomas Jefferson

We know nothing of what will happen in the future, but by the analogy of past experience.
Abraham Lincoln

The best thing about the future is that it comes only one day at a time.
Abraham Lincoln

I never think of the future. It comes soon enough.
Albert Einstein

The trouble with our times is that the future is not what it used to be.
Paul Valéry

The future is like heaven—everyone exalts it but no one wants to go there now.
James Baldwin

You can destroy your now by worrying about tomorrow.
Janis Joplin

As one went to Europe to see the living past, so one must visit California to observe the future.
Alison Lurie

Future shock is the dizzying disorientation brought on by the premature arrival of the future.
Alvin Toffler

Genius

There is no great genius without some touch of madness.
Lucius Annaeus Seneca

When a true genius appears in the world, you may know him by this sign, that the dunces are all in confederacy against him.
Jonathan Swift

Genius is patience.
Comte de Buffon

To do easily what is difficult for others is the mark of talent. To do what is impossible for talent is the mark of genius.
Henri Frédéric Amiel

Genius is mainly an affair of energy.
>> *Matthew Arnold*

Common sense is genius dressed in its working
clothes.
>> *Ralph Waldo Emerson*

Towering genius disdains a beaten path.
>> *Abraham Lincoln*

Genius is one per cent inspiration and ninety-nine
per cent perspiration.
>> *Thomas Alva Edison*

A genius is one who can do anything except make a
living.
>> *Joey Adams*

God

God is love; and he that dwelleth in love dwelleth in
God, and God in him.
>> *1 John 4:16*

Be still and know that I am God.
>> *Psalms 46:10*

God never shuts one door but He opens another.
>> *Irish proverb*

There are three things that only God knows: the beginning of things, the cause of things, and the end of
things.
>> *Welsh proverb*

He who leaves God out of his reckoning does not
know how to count.
>> *Italian proverb*

God shall be my hope, my stay, my guide, and lantern to my feet.
William Shakespeare

It is the heart which experiences God, and not the reason.
Blaise Pascal

My reason tells me that God exists, but it also tells me that I can never know what He is.
Voltaire

God moves in a mysterious way
His wonders to perform.
William Cowper

God's in His Heaven—All's right with the world.
Robert Browning

But I always think that the best way to know God is to love many things.
Vincent Van Gogh

God will forgive me; it is His trade.
Heinrich Heine

God is the poet of the world, with tender patience leading it by His vision of truth, beauty, and goodness.
Alfred North Whitehead

As a countenance is made beautiful by the soul's shining through it, so the world is beautified by the shining through it of God.
Friedrich Jacobi

Every man thinks God is on his side. The rich and powerful know He is.
> Jean Anouilh

The word of the Lord falls with the force of a snowflake.
> William Sloane Coffin

Why is it when we talk to God, we're said to be praying—but when God talks to us, we're schizophrenic?
> Lily Tomlin

Goodness

Goodness and greatness go not always together.
> John Clarke

Do good by stealth, and blush to find it fame.
> Alexander Pope

Goodness that preaches undoes itself.
> Ralph Waldo Emerson

To be good is noble; but to show others how to be good is nobler and no trouble.
> Mark Twain

A man is only as good as what he loves.
> Saul Bellow

A good man isn't good for everything.
> John W. Gardner

Grief

Every one can master a grief but he that has it.
> William Shakespeare

It is better to drink of deep griefs than to taste
shallow pleasures.
William Hazlitt

The only cure for grief is action.
George Henry Lewes

Happiness is beneficial for the body, but it is grief
that develops the powers of the mind.
Marcel Proust

Grief can't be shared. Everyone carries it alone, his
own burden, his own way.
Anne Morrow Lindbergh

Habits

The chains of habit are too weak to be felt until they
are too strong to be broken.
Samuel Johnson

Habit is stronger than reason.
George Santayana

The unfortunate thing about this world is that good
habits are so much easier to give up than bad ones.
W. Somerset Maugham

Happiness

He that keepeth the law, happy is he.
Proverbs 29:18

He that is of a merry heart hath a continual feast.
Proverbs 17:22

No man is happy unless he believes he is.
Publilius Syrus

He who goes out of his house in search of happiness runs after a shadow.

> *Chinese proverb*

The three secrets of happiness: to see no evil, to hear no evil, to do no evil.

> *Chinese proverb*

All the Constitution guarantees is the pursuit of happiness. You have to catch up with it yourself.

> *Benjamin Franklin*

Happiness is nothing more than health and a poor memory.

> *Albert Schweitzer*

Hate

Hatreds are the cinders of affection.

> *Sir Walter Raleigh*

When our hatred is too keen it places us beneath those we hate.

> *François de La Rochefoucauld*

Men hate more steadily than they love.

> *Samuel Johnson*

Hatred is the coward's revenge for being intimidated.

> *George Bernard Shaw*

If you hate a person, you hate something in him that is part of yourself. What isn't part of ourselves doesn't disturb us.

> *Hermann Hesse*

Passionate hatred can give meaning and purpose to
an empty life.
>*Eric Hoffer*

The price of hating other human beings is loving
oneself less.
>*Eldridge Cleaver*

Hero

A hero is one who knows how to hang on one
minute longer.
>*Norwegian proverb*

No man is a hero to his valet.
>*Ascribed to Madame Cornuel*

A light supper, a good night's sleep, and a fine
morning have sometimes made a hero of the same
man who, by an indigestion, a restless night, and
rainy morning would have proved a coward.
>*Lord Chesterfield*

The opportunities for heroism are limited in this kind
of world: the most people can do is sometimes not
to be as weak as they've been at other times.
>*Angus Wilson*

Each man is a hero and an oracle to somebody.
>*Ralph Waldo Emerson*

As you get older it is harder to have heroes, but it is
sort of necessary.
>*Ernest Hemingway*

History

History repeats itself.
> *English proverb*

Not to know what happened before one was born is always to be a child.
> *Cicero*

History can be well written only in a free country.
> *Voltaire*

History is a record of the gradual negation of man's original bestiality by the evolution of his humanity.
> *Mikhail Bakunin*

History, *n.* An account mostly false, of events mostly unimportant, which are brought about by rulers mostly knaves, and soldiers mostly fools.
> *Ambrose Bierce*

That men do not learn very much from the lessons of history is the most important of all the lessons that history has to teach.
> *Aldous Huxley*

You don't change the course of history by turning the faces of portraits to the wall.
> *Jawaharlal Nehru*

History never looks like history when you are living through it. It always looks confusing and messy, and it always feels uncomfortable.
> *John W. Gardner*

Honesty

In an honest man there is always something of a child.
> *Plato*

An honest man's word is as good as his bond.
> *Miguel de Cervantes*

A show of a certain amount of honesty is in any profession or business the surest way of growing rich.
> *Jean de La Bruyère*

An honest man's the noblest work of God.
> *Alexander Pope*

To make your children capable of honesty is the beginning of education.
> *John Ruskin*

No men living are more worthy to be trusted than those who toil up from poverty—nor less inclined to touch aught which they have not honestly earned.
> *Abraham Lincoln*

Nothing increases your golf score like witnesses.
> Bits & Pieces

Hope

Great hopes make great men.
> *Thomas Fuller*

If it were not for hopes, the heart would break.
> *Thomas Fuller*

If Winter comes, can Spring be far behind?
Percy Bysshe Shelley

Die when I may, I want it said of me, by those who know me best, that I always plucked a thistle and planted a flower when I thought a flower would grow.
Abraham Lincoln

There is nothing so well known as that we should not expect something for nothing—but we all do and call it Hope.
Edgar Watson Howe

Humility

The fruits of humility are love and peace.
Hebrew proverb

The higher we are placed, the more we should be humble.
Cicero

Plenty of people want to be pious, but no one yearns to be humble.
François de La Rochefoucauld

To be humble to superiors is duty, to equals courtesy, to inferiors nobleness.
Benjamin Franklin

Humility is the first of the virtues—for other people.
Oliver Wendell Holmes, Sr.

Don't be humble, you're not that great.
Golda Meir

Ideas

New ideas cannot be administered successfully by men with old ideas, for the first essential of doing a job well is the wish to see the job done at all.

Franklin D. Roosevelt

Bring ideas in and entertain them royally, for one of them may be the king.

Mark Van Doren

An idea isn't responsible for the people who believe in it.

Don Marquis

Ignorance

He who would be cured of ignorance must confess it.

Michel Eyquem de Montaigne

He that knows least commonly presumes most.

Thomas Fuller

. . . where ignorance is bliss
'Tis folly to be wise.

Thomas Gray

No one is exempt from talking nonsense; the mistake is to do it solemnly.

Michel Eyquem de Montaigne

If a nation expects to be ignorant and free, in a state of civilization, it expects what never was and never will be.

Thomas Jefferson

How exactly proportioned to a man's ignorance of the subject is the noise he makes about it at a public meeting.
Sir Arthur Helps

The wisest thing to do with a fool is to encourage him to hire a hall and discourse to his fellow citizens. Nothing chills nonsense like exposure to the air.
Woodrow Wilson

Everybody is ignorant, only on different subjects.
Will Rogers

If ignorance paid dividends most Americans could make a fortune out of what they don't know about economics.
Luther Hodges

Immortality

Surely God would not have created such a being as man, with an ability to grasp the infinite, to exist only for a day! No, no, man was made for immortality.
Abraham Lincoln

I don't want to achieve immortality through my work, I want to achieve immortality through not dying.
Woody Allen

Indifference

Nothing is more conducive to peace of mind than not having any opinion at all.
Georg Christoph Lichtenberg

Most of us have no real loves and no real hatreds. Blessed is love, less blessed is hatred, but thrice accursed is that indifference which is neither one nor the other.

Mark Rutherford

The worst sin towards our fellow creatures is not to hate them, but to be indifferent to them: that's the essence of inhumanity.

George Bernard Shaw

Many a deep secret that cannot be pried out by curiosity can be drawn out by indifference.

Sydney J. Harris

To try may be to die, but not to care is never to be born.

William Redfield

The accomplice to the crime of corruption is frequently our own indifference.

Bess Myerson

Individual

If a man does not keep pace with his companions, perhaps it is because he hears a different drummer. Let him step to the music he hears, however measured or far away.

Henry David Thoreau

That cause is strong, which has not a multitude, but one strong man behind it.

James Russell Lowell

Any power must be the enemy of mankind which enslaves the individual by terror and force, whether it arises under a Fascist or Communist flag. All that is valuable in human society depends upon the opportunity for development accorded to the individual.
Albert Einstein

Men are born equal but they are also born different.
Erich Fromm

The best things and best people rise out of their separateness; I'm against a homogenized society because I want the cream to rise.
Robert Frost

Individualism is rather like innocence; there must be something unconscious about it.
Louis Kronenberger

Inequality

Though all men were made of one metal, yet they were not cast all in the same mold.
Thomas Fuller

Whenever there is great property, there is great inequality . . . for one very rich man, there must be at least five hundred poor.
Adam Smith

Whatever may be the general endeavor of a community to render its members equal and alike, the personal pride of individuals will always seek to rise above the line, and to form somewhere an inequality to their own advantage.
Alexis de Tocqueville

All animals are equal, but some animals are more equal than others.
> George Orwell

While there is a lower class I am in it, while there is a criminal element I am of it, and while there is a soul in prison I am not free.
> Eugene Debs

Influence

He who goes with wolves learns to howl.
> Spanish proverb

The rotten apple spoils his companions.
> Benjamin Franklin

A teacher affects eternity; he can never tell where his influence stops.
> Henry Brooks Adams

One of the things a man has to learn to fight most bitterly is the influence of those who love him.
> Sherwood Anderson

Human beings are not influenced by anything to which they are not naturally disposed.
> Hesketh Pearson

Inspiration

No man was ever great without some portion of divine inspiration.
> Cicero

We cannot carry on inspiration and make it consecutive. One day there is no electricity in the air, and the next the world bristles with sparks like a cat's back.

> *Ralph Waldo Emerson*

Inspiration is a farce that poets have invented to give themselves importantce.

> *Jean Anouilh*

My sole inspiration is a telephone call from a producer.

> *Cole Porter*

Integrity

The just man walketh in his integrity.

> *Proverbs 20:7*

This above all: to thine own self be true,
And it must follow, as the night the day,
Thou canst not then be false to any man.

> *William Shakespeare*

Nothing so completely baffles one who is full of trick and duplicity himself, than straightforward and simple integrity in another.

> *Charles Caleb Colton*

It is better to be hated for what you are than loved for what you are not.

> *André Gide*

To be individually righteous is the first of all duties, come what may to one's self, to one's country, to society, and to civilization itself.

> *Joseph Wood Krutch*

Justice

All virtue is summed up in dealing justly.
Aristotle

Justice is the crowning glory of the virtues.
Cicero

The aim of justice is to give everyone his due.
Cicero

Justice is the end of government.
Daniel Defoe

Rigid justice is the greatest injustice.
Thomas Fuller

Justice is truth in action.
Joseph Joubert

It is impossible to be just if one is not generous.
Joseph Roux

There is no such thing as justice—in or out of court.
Clarence Darrow

Justice delayed is democracy denied.
Robert Francis Kennedy

To have true justice we must have equal harrassment
under the law.
Paul Krassner

Let lawmakers, judges and lawyers think less of the
law and more of justice.
Phillip Berrigan

Knowledge

When you know a thing, to hold that you know it, and when you do not know it, to admit that you do not—this is true knowledge.
Confucius

The fear of the Lord is the beginning of knowledge.
Proverbs 1:7

He that increaseth knowledge increaseth sorrow.
Ecclesiastes 1:18

All wish to know, but none want to pay the price.
Juvenal

Whoever acquires knowledge and does not practice it resembles him who ploughs his land and leaves it unsown.
Saadi

Knowledge is power.
Francis Bacon

A little learning is a dangerous thing;
Drink deep, or taste not the Pierian spring:
There shallow draughts intoxicate the brain,
And drinking largely sobers us again.
Alexander Pope

If a little knowledge is dangerous, where is the man who has so much as to be out of danger?
Thomas Henry Huxley

You know you've read a good book when you turn the last page and feel a little as if you have lost a friend.
Paul Sweeney

Law

The law is reason free from passion.
Aristotle

Good men need no laws, and bad men are not made better by them.
Ascribed to Demonax of Cyprus

The purpose of law is to prevent the strong always having their way.
Ovid

Wherever law ends, tyranny begins.
John Locke

Were we to act but in cases where no contrary opinion of a lawyer can be had, we should never act.
Thomas Jefferson

Ignorance of the law is no excuse in any country. If it were, the laws would lose their effect, because it can be always pretended.
Thomas Jefferson

If there were not bad people there would be no good lawyers.
Charles Dickens

Nothing should ever be implied as law which leads to unjust or absurd consequences.
Abraham Lincoln

Nobody has a more sacred obligation to obey the law than those who make the law.
Jean Anouilh

There are not enough jails, not enough policemen, not enough courts to enforce a law not supported by the people.

Hubert H. Humphrey

Law is the indispensable attribute of an ordered society.

Elliot Richardson

The law protects everybody who can afford to hire a good lawyer.

Author unknown

Liberty

Liberty plucks justice by the nose.

William Shakespeare

I have sworn upon the altar of God eternal hostility against every form of tyranny over the mind of men.

Thomas Jefferson

I know not what course others may take, but as for me, give me liberty, or give me death!

Patrick Henry

Liberty is obedience to the law which one has laid down for oneself.

Jean Jacques Rousseau

Liberty means responsibility. That is why most men dread it.

George Bernard Shaw

Liberty don't work as good in practice as it does in Speech.

Will Rogers

I am a lover of my own liberty and so I would do nothing to restrict yours.
Mohandas K. Gandhi

Life

Life is a theatre in which the worst people often have the best seats.
Ascribed to Aristonymus

Life is long to the miserable, but short to the happy.
Publilius Syrus

The art of living is more like wrestling than dancing.
Marcus Aurelius

We are born crying, live complaining, and die disappointed.
Thomas Fuller

Life is a jest, and all things show it;
I thought so once, and now I know it.
John Gay

To most of us the real life is the life we do not lead.
Oscar Wilde

Life is one long process of getting tired.
Samuel Butler

Life is a long lesson in humility.
Sir James Matthew Barrie

Life is too short for men to take it seriously.
George Bernard Shaw

The basic fact about human existence is not that it is a tragedy, but that it is a bore. It is not so much a war as an endless standing in line.

    H. L. Mencken

Life is like an onion: you peel it off one layer at a time, and sometimes you weep.

    Carl Sandburg

I never lose sight of the fact that just *being* is fun.

    Katharine Hepburn

Love

In love, there is always one who kisses and one who offers the cheek.

    French proverb

It is impossible to love and be wise.

    Francis Bacon

Love is an image of God, and not a lifeless image, but the living essence of the divine nature which beams full of all goodness.

    Martin Luther

Love your neighbor—but don't pull down your hedge.

    Benjamin Franklin

The first sigh of love is the last of wisdom.

    Antoine Bret

The magic of first love is our ignorance that it can never end.

    Benjamin Disraeli

Men always want to be a woman's first love—
women like to be a man's last romance.
Oscar Wilde

Anything will give up its secrets if you love it
enough.
George Washington Carver

Love cures people—both the ones who give it and
the ones who receive it.
Dr. Karl Menninger

Love dies only when growth stops.
Pearl S. Buck

In love the paradox occurs that two beings become
one and yet remain two.
Erich Fromm

There is hardly any activity, any enterprise, which is
started with such tremendous hopes and expecta-
tions, and yet which fails so regularly, as love.
Erich Fromm

Man

A truly great man never puts away the simplicity of a
child.
Confucius

Men, in general, are but great children.
Napoleon I

If you pick up a starving dog and make him prosperous, he will not bite you. That is the principal
difference between a dog and a man.
Mark Twain

No man who is occupied in doing a very difficult thing, and doing it very well, ever loses his self-respect.

George Bernard Shaw

A man who has no office to go to—I don't care who he is—is a trial of which you can have no conception.

George Bernard Shaw

Men build bridges and throw railroads across deserts, and yet they contend successfully that the job of sewing on a button is beyond them.

Heywood Broun

Manliness is not all swagger and swearing and mountain climbing. Manliness is also tenderness, gentleness, consideration.

Robert Anderson

They say women talk too much. If you have worked in Congress you know that the filibuster was invented by men.

Clare Boothe Luce

Men don't understand, as a rule, that women like to get used to them by degrees.

John Oliver Hobbes

Mankind

Men's natures are alike; it is their habits that carry them far apart.

Confucius

Any man's death diminishes me because I am involved in mankind.

John Donne

In general, mankind, since the improvement of
cookery, eats twice as much as nature requires.
   Benjamin Franklin

Human nature will not change. In any future great
national trial, compared with the men of this, we
shall have as weak and as strong, as silly and as
wise, as bad and as good.
   Abraham Lincoln

Man is a gregarious animal, and much more so in
his mind than in his body. He may like to go alone
for a walk, but he hates to stand alone in his opinions.
   George Santayana

Man is the only animal that blushes. Or needs to.
   Mark Twain

The old believe everything. The middle-aged suspect
everything. The young know everything.
   Oscar Wilde

Marriage

It is mind, not body, that makes marriage last.
   Publilius Syrus

Keep thy eyes wide open before marriage, and half
shut afterwards.
   Benjamin Franklin

Marry your own son when you will, your daughter
when you can.
   Benjamin Franklin

It doesn't much signify whom one marries, for one is sure to find next morning that it was someone else.
    Samuel Rogers

Men marry because they are tired, women because they are curious. Both are disappointed.
    Oscar Wilde

I learned a great many years ago that in a fight between a man and his wife, a third person should never get between the woman's rolling pin and the man's boot.
    Franklin D. Roosevelt

Married and unmarried women waste a great deal of time in feeling sorry for each other.
    Myrtle Reed

A man who marries a woman to educate her falls a victim to the same fallacy as the woman who marries a man to reform him.
    Elbert Hubbard

The dread of loneliness is greater than the fear of bondage, so we get married.
    Cyril Connolly

Before marriage, a man declares that he would lay down his life to serve you; after marriage, he won't even lay down his newspaper to talk to you.
    Helen Rowland

Marrying a man is like buying something you've been admiring for a long time in a shop window. You may love it when you get home, but it doesn't always go with everything else in the house.
    Jean Kerr

We sleep in separate rooms, we have dinner apart, we take separate vacations—we're doing everything we can to keep our marriage together.
> *Rodney Dangerfield*

Marriage, in life, is like a duel in the midst of a battle.
> *Edmond About*

A successful marriage is not a gift; it is an achievement.
> *Ann Landers*

Mercy

In case of doubt it is best to lean to the side of mercy.
> *Legal maxim*

The merciful man doeth good to his own soul.
> *Proverbs 11:17*

It is impossible to imagine anything which better becomes a ruler than mercy.
> *Marcus Annaeus Seneca*

The quality of mercy is not strained;
It droppeth as the gentle rain from heaven
Upon the place beneath. It is twice blessed—
It blesseth him that gives, and him that takes.
> *William Shakespeare*

We hand folks over to God's mercy, and show none ourselves.
> *George Eliot*

Mind

The mind covers more ground than the heart but
goes less far.
Chinese proverb

It is good to run and polish your mind against the
minds of others.
Michel Eyquem de Montaigne

Minds differ still more than faces.
Voltaire

I think there is only one quality worse than hardness
of heart and that is softness of head.
Theodore Roosevelt

Men are not prisoners of fate, but only prisoners of
their own minds.
Franklin Delano Roosevelt

We should take care not to make the intellect our
god; it has, of course, powerful muscles, but no per-
sonality.
Albert Einstein

Unfortunately, I have an open mind. I let down a
window in my brain about six or seven inches from
the top even in the bitterest weather.
Heywood Broun

Many creatures have brains. Man alone has mind.
Buckminster Fuller

The mind is like a clock that is constantly running
down; it has to be wound up daily with good
thoughts.
Fulton J. Sheen

Money

If rich people could hire other people to die for them, the poor could make a wonderful living.
> Yiddish proverb

The love of money is the root of all evil.
> 1 Timothy 6:10

Money makes not so many true friends as real enemies.
> Thomas Fuller

He that is of opinion money will do everything may well be suspected of doing everything for money.
> Benjamin Franklin

I'm opposed to millionaires, but it would be dangerous to offer me the position.
> Mark Twain

Money does not make you happy but it quiets the nerves.
> Sean O'Casey

If you would know what the Lord God thinks of money, you have only to look at those to whom he gives it.
> Maurice Baring

The man who damns money has obtained it dishonorably; the man who respects it has earned it.
> Ayn Rand

There was a time when a fool and his money were soon parted, but now it happens to everybody.
> Adlai E. Stevenson II

I finally know what distinguishes man from the other beasts: financial worries.

> Jules Renard

The more money an American accumulates, the less interesting he becomes.

> Gore Vidal

People call it take-home pay because there is no other place you can afford to go with it.

> Philadelphia Evening Bulletin

Morality

Be not too hasty to trust or to admire the teachers of morality: they discourse like angels, but they live like men.

> Samuel Johnson

If only a tenth part of the morality that is in books existed in the heart!

> Georg Christoph Lichtenberg

If your morals make you dreary, depend upon it, they are wrong.

> Robert Louis Stevenson

It is not best that we use our morals week days; it gets them out of repair for Sundays.

> Mark Twain

What is moral is what you feel good after and what is immoral is what you feel bad after.

> Ernest Hemingway

The only immorality is to not do what one has to do when one has to do it.

> Jean Anouilh

Mother

God could not be everywhere, so he made mothers.
The Talmud

In the eyes of its mother every beetle is a gazelle.
Moroccan proverb

Mother is the name of God in the lips and hearts of
little children.
William Makepeace Thackeray

The mother's heart is the child's schoolroom.
Henry Ward Beecher

The hand that rocks the cradle is the hand that rules
the world.
W. R. Wallace

A mother is not a person to lean on, but a person to
make leaning unnecessary.
Dorothy Canfield Harrison

No matter how old a mother is she watches her
middle-aged children for signs of improvement.
Florida Scott-Maxwell

Nation

The ruin of a nation begins in the homes of its
people.
Ashanti proverb

A nation never falls but by suicide.
Ralph Waldo Emerson

Individualities may form communities, but it is institutions alone that can create a nation.
Benjamin Disraeli

71

We can afford to exercise the self-restraint of a really great nation which realizes its own strength and scorns to misuse it.

Woodrow Wilson

Men may be linked in friendship. Nations are linked only by interests.

Rolf Hochhuth

Nations, like individuals, have to limit their objectives, or take the consequences.

James Reston

Nature

Those things are better which are perfected by nature than those which are finished by art.

Cicero

Nature is the art of God.

Dante Alighieri

Let us permit nature to have her way: she understands her business better than we do.

Michel Eyquem de Montaigne

Nature, to be commanded, must be obeyed.

Francis Bacon

Nature seldom gives us the very best; for that we must have recourse to art.

Baltasar Gracián

Nature never quite goes along with us. She is sombre at weddings, sunny at funerals, and she frowns on ninety-nine out of a hundred picnics.

Alexander Smith

Man masters nature not by force but by understanding.
>   *Jacob Bronowski*

Obedience

Learn to obey before you command.
>   *Solon*

He who obeys with modesty will be worthy some
day of being allowed to command.
>   *Cicero*

The man who does something under orders is not
unhappy; he is unhappy who does something against
his will.
>   *Marcus Annaeus Seneca*

Let them obey that know not how to rule.
>   *William Shakespeare*

The height of ability in the least able consists in
knowing how to submit to the good leadership of
others.
>   *François de La Rochefoucauld*

Old Age

Withered trees in spring burst forth afresh; but men
cannot be young twice.
>   *Chinese proverb*

No one is so old that he does not think he could live
another year.
>   *Cicero*

Old men like to give good advice in order to console themselves for not being any longer able to set bad examples.

    François de La Rochefoucauld

We hope to grow old, and yet we dread old age.

    Jean de La Bruyère

As we grow old, . . . the beauty steals inward.

    Ralph Waldo Emerson

Before you contradict an old man, my fair friend, you should endeavour to understand him.

    George Santayana

To me, old age is always fifteen years older than I am.

    Bernard Baruch

Old age isn't so bad when you consider the alternative.

    Maurice Chevalier

You're never too old to become younger.

    Mae West

Old age is like everything else. To make a success of it, you've got to start young.

    Fred Astaire

Opinion

We credit scarcely any persons with good sense except those who are of our opinion.

    François de La Rochefoucauld

I am quite capable of defending an opinion, but I cannot choose one.
Michel Eyquem de Montaigne

New opinions are always suspected, and usually opposed, without any other reason but because they are not already common.
John Locke

One must judge men not by their opinions, but by what their opinions have made of them.
Georg Christoph Lichtenberg

A man's opinions are generally of much more value than his arguments.
Oliver Wendell Holmes, Sr.

It were not best that we should all think alike; it is difference of opinion that makes horse-races.
Mark Twain

We tolerate differences of opinion in people who are familiar to us. But differences of opinion in people we do not know sound like heresy or plots.
Brooks Atkinson

Pain

An hour of pain is as long as a day of pleasure.
English proverb

Who, except the gods, can live time through forever without any pain?
Aeschylus

Those who do not feel pain seldom think that it is felt.

Samuel Johnson

He preaches patience that never knew pain.

H. G. Bohn

To render ourselves insensible to pain we must forfeit also the possibility of happiness.

Sir John Lubbock

Pain and death are a part of life. To reject them is to reject life itself.

Havelock Ellis

Pain makes man think. Thought makes man wise. Wisdom makes life endurable.

John Patrick

Parents

We never know the love of our parents for us till we have become parents.

Henry Ward Beecher

Where parents do too much for their children, the children will not do much for themselves.

Elbert Hubbard

Parents are the bones on which children cut their teeth.

Peter Ustinov

We get our parents at so late an age that it is impossible to change their habits.

Boston Evening Transcript

Patience

A journey of a thousand miles began with a single step.
> *Lao Tsu*

Patience is a bitter plant but it has sweet fruit.
> *German proverb*

How poor are they that have not patience.
What wound did ever heal but by degrees?
> *William Shakespeare*

All commend patience, but none can endure to suffer.
> *Thomas Fuller*

He that can have patience can have what he will.
> *Benjamin Franklin*

Patience is bitter, but its fruits are sweet.
> *Jean Jacques Rousseau*

Our patience will achieve more than our force.
> *Edmund Burke*

You can't set a hen in one morning and have chicken salad for lunch.
> *George Humphrey*

Peace

Peace is liberty in tranquility.
> *Cicero*

'Tis safest making peace with sword in hand.
> *George Farquhar*

It is madness for a sheep to treat of peace with a
wolf.
>   *Thomas Fuller*

Peace hath higher tests of manhood
Than battle ever knew.
>   *John Greenleaf Whittier*

If peace cannot be maintained with honor, it is no
longer peace.
>   *Lord John Russell*

We are going to have peace even if we have to fight
for it.
>   *Dwight David Eisenhower*

Arms alone are not enough to keep the peace. It
must be kept by men.
>   *John Fitzgerald Kennedy*

If you want to make peace, you don't talk to your
friends. You talk to your enemies.
>   *Moshe Dayan*

Perseverance

The probability that we may fail in the struggle ought
not to deter us from the support of a cause we believe to be just.
>   *Abraham Lincoln*

When you get to the end of your rope, tie a knot
and hang on.
>   *Franklin D. Roosevelt*

Perseverance: stubbornness put to good use.
>   Wall Street Journal

78

Philosophy

The beginning of philosophy is the recognition of the conflict between opinions.

Epictetus

Even a mole may instruct a philosopher in the art of digging.

Chinese proverb

Wonder is the foundation of all philosophy, inquiry the progress, ignorance the end.

Michel Eyquem de Montaigne

To make light of philosophy is to be a true philosopher.

Blaise Pascal

The first step toward philosophy is incredulity.

Denis Diderot

All philosophies, if you ride them home, are nonsense; but some are greater nonsense than others.

Samuel Butler

Let there be no inscription upon my tomb. Let no man write my epitaph. Let my character and motives repose in security and peace until other times and other men can do them justice.

Robert Emmet

The object of studying philosophy is to know one's own mind, not other people's.

William Ralph Inge

I have looked into the most philosophical systems, and have found none that will work without a God.

James Clerk Maxwell

If the only tool you have is a hammer, you tend to see every problem as a nail.
Abraham Maslow

Pleasure

There is no such thing as pure pleasure; some anxiety always goes with it.
Ovid

Do not bite at the bait of pleasure till you know there is no hook beneath it.
Thomas Jefferson

Most men pursue pleasure with such breathless haste that they hurry past it.
Søren Kierkegaard

Do you know the only thing that gives me pleasure? It's to see my dividends coming in.
John D. Rockefeller

The great pleasure in life is doing what people say you cannot do.
Walter Bagehot

There are two things to aim at in life; first, to get what you want; and, after that, to enjoy it. Only the wisest of mankind achieve the second.
Logan Pearsall Smith

Mankind is safer when men seek pleasure than when they seek the power and the glory.
Geoffrey Gorer

People seem to enjoy things more when they know a lot of other people have been left out of the pleasure.
Russell Baker

Politics

The good of man must be the end of the science of politics.
Aristotle

Politics is the doctrine of the possible, the attainable.
Otto von Bismarck

Politics is perhaps the only profession for which no preparation is thought necessary.
Robert Louis Stevenson

The politician is an acrobat. He keeps his balance by saying the opposite of what he does.
Maurice Barrès

When the political columnists say "Every thinking man" they mean themselves, and when the candidates appeal to "every intelligent voter" they mean everybody who is going to vote for them.
Franklin P. Adams

The most successful politician is he who says what everybody is thinking most often and in the loudest voice.
Theodore Roosevelt

I have sometimes heard men say politics must have nothing to do with business, and I have often wished that business had nothing to do with politics.
Woodrow Wilson

If you think too much about being reelected, it is very difficult to be worth reelecting.
Woodrow Wilson

81

We would help to cure senility and seniority—both terrible legislative diseases nationally—if twelve years were the limit of service for President, senators, and congressmen.

> Harry Truman

Politics are almost as exciting as war, and quite as dangerous. In war, you can only be killed once, but in politics many times.

> Sir Winston Churchill

Other employees would do no better than Congressmen if the boss showed an interest in them only once in two years.

> Unknown

Power

The sole advantage of power is that you can do more good.

> Baltasar Gracián

In the general course of human nature, a power over a man's subsistence amounts to a power over his will.

> Alexander Hamilton

The highest proof of virtue is to possess boundless power without abusing it.

> Thomas Babington Macaulay

Power tends to corrupt and absolute power corrupts absolutely.

> Lord Acton

Power does not corrupt men; fools, however, if they get into a position of power, corrupt power.

> George Bernard Shaw

The only prize much cared for by the powerful is power. The prize of the general is not a bigger tent, but command.
Oliver Wendell Holmes, Jr.

Every successful revolution puts on in time the robes of the tyrant it has deposed.
Barbara Tuchman

The problem of power is how to achieve its responsible use rather than its irresponsible and indulgent use—of how to get men of power to live for the public rather than off the public.
Robert Francis Kennedy

Praise

He who refuses praise only wants to be praised again.
François de La Rochefoucauld

There's no praise to beat the sort you can put in your pocket.
Molière

Pride

Never be boastful; someone may come along who knew you as a child.
Chinese proverb

Pride goeth before destruction, and a haughty spirit before a fall.
Proverbs 16:18

The proud hate pride—in others.
Benjamin Franklin

Pride is at the bottom of all great mistakes.
> John Ruskin

All the extraordinary men I have ever known were
chiefly extraordinary in their own estimation.
> Woodrow Wilson

Progress

Progress might have been all right once, but it's gone
on too long.
> Ogden Nash

Prudence

No one tests the depth of a river with both feet.
> Ashanti proverb

He that fights and runs away
Will live to fight another day.
> Old English rhyme

Consider the little mouse, how sagacious an animal
it is which never entrusts its life to one hole only.
> Plautus

The better part of valour is discretion.
> William Shakespeare

Love all, trust a few, do wrong to none.
> William Shakespeare

If thou thinkest twice before thou speakest once,
thou wilt speak twice the better for it.
> William Penn

Don't judge a man's wealth—or his piety—by his
appearance on Sunday.
>   *Benjamin Franklin*

Never buy what you do not want, because it is
cheap; it will be dear to you.
>   *Thomas Jefferson*

Put all your eggs in one basket—and watch that
basket.
>   *Mark Twain*

If Noah had been truly wise, he would have swatted
those two flies.
>   *Helen Castle*

Quality

Good things cost less than bad ones.
>   *Italian proverb*

We should not judge of a man's merits by his great
qualities, but by the use he makes of them.
>   *François de La Rochefoucauld*

A man has generally the good or ill qualities which
he attributes to mankind.
>   *William Shenstone*

Nothing endures but noble qualities.
>   *Walt Whitman*

Reason

Reason is the wise man's guide, example the fool's.
>   *Welsh proverb*

Swift instinct leaps; slow reason feebly climbs.
Edward Young

We may take Fancy for a companion, but must
follow Reason as our guide.
Samuel Johnson

The man who listens to Reason is lost: Reason enslaves all whose minds are not strong enough to
master her.
George Bernard Shaw

Religion

It is when we are in misery that we revere the gods;
the prosperous seldom approach the altar.
Silius Italicus

Nature teaches us to love our friends, but religion
our enemies.
Thomas Fuller

If men are so wicked with religion, what would they
be without it?
Benjamin Franklin

It does me no injury for my neighbor to say there are
twenty Gods or no God. It neither picks my pocket
nor breaks my leg.
Thomas Jefferson

The effect of the coercion [of Christianity] has been
to make one half of the world fools and the other
half hypocrites.
Thomas Jefferson

Nothing is so fatal to religion as indifference.
Edmund Burke

A religion without mystery must be a religion
without God.
    Jeremy Taylor

What a pity it is that we have no amusements in England but vice and religion.
    Sidney Smith

In my religion there would be no exclusive doctrine;
all would be love, poetry and doubt.
    Cyril Connolly

Religion is a candle inside a multicolored lantern.
Everyone looks through a particular color, but the
candle is always there.
    Muhammad Naguib

All God's religions . . . have not been able to put
mankind back together again.
    John Cage

If you can't joke about your religion, you're not
steadfast in your piety—you're simply afflicted with
the disease of "religiosity."
    Sydney J. Harris

Responsibility

Responsibility, *n.* A detachable burden easily shifted
to the shoulders of God, Fate, Fortune, Luck or one's
neighbor. In the days of astrology it was customary
to unload it upon a star.
    Ambrose Bierce

Man's responsibility increases as that of the gods decreases.
    André Gide

It is our responsibilities, not ourselves, that we
should take seriously.
    Peter Ustinov

Few things help an individual more than to place responsibility upon him, and to let him know that you
trust him.
    Booker T. Washington

Sacrifice

Greater love hath no man than this, that a man lay
down his life for his friends.
    John 15:13

Self-sacrifice enables us to sacrifice other people
without blushing.
    George Bernard Shaw

The mice which helplessly find themselves between
the cat's teeth acquire no merit from their enforced
sacrifice.
    Mohandas K. Gandhi

What do the dangers or sacrifices of a man matter
when the destiny of humanity is at stake?
    Ché Guevara

Service

The charity that is a trifle to us can be precious to
others.
    Homer

They also serve who only stand and wait.
    John Milton

The fragrance always stays in the hand that gives the rose.
Hada Bejar

The noblest service comes from nameless hands,
And the best servant does his work unseen.
Oliver Wendell Holmes, Sr.

A large part of altruism, even when it is perfectly honest, is grounded upon the fact that it is uncomfortable to have unhappy people about one.
H. L. Mencken

Solitude

He never is alone that is accompanied with noble thoughts.
Francis Beaumont and John Fletcher

I would rather sit on a pumpkin and have it all to myself than be crowded on a velvet cushion.
Henry David Thoreau

The person who tries to live alone will not succeed as a human being. His heart withers if it does not answer another heart. His mind shrinks away if he hears only the echoes of his own thoughts and finds no other inspiration.
Pearl S. Buck

Sorrow

He truly sorrows who sorrows unseen.
Martial

When sorrows come, they come not single spies,
But in battalions.
William Shakespeare

When a man or woman loves to brood over a
sorrow and takes care to keep it green in their
memory, you may be sure it is no longer a pain to
them.
>   Jerome K. Jerome

One cannot be deeply responsive to the world
without being saddened very often.
>   Erich Fromm

Soul

What shall it profit a man, if he shall gain the whole
world, and lose his own soul?
>   Mark 8:36

There is one spectacle grander than the sea, that is
the sky: there is one spectacle grander than the sky,
that is the interior of the soul.
>   Victor Hugo

It is with the soul that we grasp the essence of another human being, not with the mind, not even
with the heart.
>   Henry Miller

State

The state exists for the sake of a good life, and not
for the sake of life only.
>   Aristotle

A state without some means of change is without the
means of its conservation.
>   Edmund Burke

The State is made for man, not man for the State.
>   Albert Einstein

90

The responsibility of great states is to serve and not to dominate the world.
    Harry S. Truman

The modern state no longer has anything but rights; it does not recognize duties any more.
    Georges Bernanos

Speeches

The more you say, the less people remember.
    Anatole France

Amplification is the vice of modern oratory. It is an insult to an assembly of reasonable men, disgusting and revolting instead of persuading. Speeches measured by the hour die by the hour.
    Thomas Jefferson

My one claim to originality among Irishmen is that I have never made a speech.
    George Moore

Strength

These three things deplete man's strength: fear, travel, and sin.
    Hebrew proverb

It is excellent
To have a giant's strength, but it is
    tyrannous
To use it like a giant.
    William Shakespeare

What is strength without a double share of wisdom?
    John Milton

That cause is strong which has not a multitude, but one strong man behind it.
James Russell Lowell

If we are strong, our character will speak for itself. If we are weak, words will be of no help.
John Fitzgerald Kennedy

Success

If you wish to succeed, consult three old people.
Chinese proverb

The way to secure success is to be more anxious about obtaining than about deserving it.
William Hazlitt

Always bear in mind that your own resolution to succeed is more important than any other one thing.
Abraham Lincoln

You cannot push anyone up the ladder unless he is willing to climb himself.
Andrew Carnegie

The man with a new idea is a crank until the idea succeeds.
Mark Twain

All you need in this life is ignorance and confidence, and then success is sure.
Mark Twain

Success covers a multitude of blunders.
George Bernard Shaw

The key to success isn't much good until one discovers the right lock to insert it in.
> *Tehyi Hsieh*

Nothing recedes like success.
> *Walter Winchell*

I don't know the key to success, but the key to failure is trying to please everybody.
> *Bill Cosby*

The fastest way to succeed is to look as if you're playing by other people's rules while quietly playing by your own.
> *Michael Korda*

If at first you do succeed—try to hide your astonishment.
> Los Angeles Times Syndicate

Suffering

He who fears he shall suffer, already suffers what he fears.
> *Michel Eyquem de Montaigne*

We are healed of a suffering only by experiencing it to the full.
> *Marcel Proust*

It is not true that suffering ennobles the character; happiness does that sometimes, but suffering, for the most part, makes men petty and vindictive.
> *W. Somerset Maugham*

Most people get a fair amount of fun out of their lives, but on balance life is suffering, and only the very young or the very foolish imagine otherwise.
George Orwell

Sympathy

When you live next to the cemetery, you cannot weep for everyone.
Russian proverb

We are fond of each other because our ailments are the same.
Jonathan Swift

Teach me to feel another's woe,
To hide the fault I see:
That mercy I to others show,
That mercy show to me.
Alexander Pope

When you are in trouble, people who call to sympathize are really looking for the particulars.
Edgar Watson Howe

Talent

No one respects a talent that is concealed.
Desiderius Erasmus

There is hardly anybody good for everything, and there is scarcely anybody who is absolutely good for nothing.
Lord Chesterfield

Everyone has a talent, what is rare is the courage to follow the talent to the dark place where it leads.
Erica Jong

Taxes

The reward of energy, enterprise, and thrift is taxes.
William Feather

Death and taxes may always be with us, but death at least doesn't get any worse.
Los Angeles Times Syndicate

Next to being shot at and missed, nothing is really quite as satisfying as an income tax refund.
F. J. Raymond

Technology

It is said that one machine can do the work of fifty ordinary men. No machine, however, can do the work of one extraordinary man.
Tehyi Hsieh

Electronic calculators can solve problems which the man who made them cannot solve; but no government-subsidized commission of engineers and physicists could create a worm.
Joseph Wood Krutch

If there is technological advance without social advance, there is, almost automatically, an increase in human misery.
Michael Harrington

Technology was developed to prevent exhausting labor. It is now dedicated to trivial conveniences.
B. F. Skinner

We shall have a race of men who are strong on telemetry and space communications but who cannot read anything but a blueprint or write anything but a computer program.
John Kenneth Galbraith

Thought

Our life is what our thoughts make it.
Marcus Aurelius

I think; therefore I am.
René Descartes

The secret thoughts of a man run over all things, holy, profane, clean, obscene, grave, and light, without shame or blame.
Thomas Hobbes

Great thoughts come from the heart.
Marquis de Vauvenargues

Where all think alike, no one thinks very much.
Walter Lippman

Time

To him who waits, time opens every door.
Chinese proverb

To one full of expectation, a moment seems a year.
Chinese proverb

Time heals what reason cannot.
    Lucius Annaeus Seneca

No person will have occasion to complain of the
want of time who never loses any.
    Thomas Jefferson

But at my back I always hear
Time's wingèd chariot hurrying near.
    Andrew Marvell

Time is money.
    Benjamin Franklin

Half our life is spent trying to find something to do
with the time we have rushed through life trying to
save.
    Will Rogers

If it weren't for the last minute, a lot of things
wouldn't get done.
    Michael S. Traylor

Travel

The shortest distance between two points is under
construction.
    Noelie Alito

This summer one third of the nation will be ill-
housed, ill-nourished and ill-clad. Only they call it a
vacation.
    Joseph Salak

Trust

Do not trust the man who tells you all his troubles
but keeps from you his joys.
> *Hebrew proverb*

Love all, trust a few.
> *William Shakespeare*

A man who doesn't trust himself can never really
trust anyone else.
> *Cardinal de Retz*

Trust thyself only, and another shall not betray thee.
> *Thomas Fuller*

Truth

Those who know the truth are not equal to those
who love it.
> *Confucius*

Who lies for you will lie against you.
> *Bosnian proverb*

Advertisements contain the only truths to be relied
on in a newspaper.
> *Thomas Jefferson*

Truth often suffers more by the heat of its defenders
than from the arguments of its opposers.
> *William Penn*

Truth is generally the best vindication against
slander.
> *Abraham Lincoln*

It is hard to believe that a man is telling the truth when you know that you would lie if you were in his place.

> H. L. Mencken

I don't want any yes-men around me. I want everyone to tell me the truth—even though it costs him his job.

> Samuel Goldwyn

Understanding

Nothing can be loved or hated unless it is first known.

> Leonardo da Vinci

Perfect understanding will sometimes almost extinguish pleasure.

> A. E. Housman

Can we understand at all, ever, where we do not love?

> Sherwood Anderson

Valor

The better part of valour is discretion.

> William Shakespeare

True valor lies in the middle, between cowardice and rashness.

> Miguel de Cervantes

Perfect valor is to do without witnesses what one would do before all the world.

> François de La Rochefoucauld

Value

Men understand the work of blessings only when
they have lost them.
Plautus

We never know the worth of water till the well is
dry.
Thomas Fuller

Try not to become a man of success but rather try to
become a man of value.
Albert Einstein

Nothing is instrinsically valuable; the value of everything is attributed to it, assigned to it from outside
the thing itself, by people.
John Barth

Variety

As land is improved by sowing it with various seeds
so is the mind by exercising it with different studies.
Pliny the Elder

Variety's the very spice of life.
William Cowper

They are the weakest-minded and the hardest
hearted man, that most love variety and change.
John Ruskin

Victory

It is no doubt a good thing to conquer on the field of
battle, but it needs greater wisdom and greater skill
to make use of victory.
Polybius

When in doubt, win the trick.
Edmond Hoyle

The god of Victory is said to be one-handed, but Peace gives victory to both sides.
Ralph Waldo Emerson

The problems of victory are more agreeable than those of defeat, but they are not less difficult.
Sir Winston Churchill

When you win, nothing hurts.
Joe Namath

Virtue

The smallest desire to do good is, though unseen by man, certainly known to Heaven.
Chinese proverb

The superior man thinks always of virtue; the common man thinks of comfort. Virtue is more clearly shown in the performance of fine actions than in the nonperformance of base ones.
Aristotle

Virtue is its own reward.
Cicero

When men grow virtuous in their old age, they only make a sacrifice to God of the devil's leavings.
Jonathan Swift

No virtue is ever so strong that it is beyond temptation.
Immanuel Kant

The measure of any man's virtue is what he would do, if he had neither the laws or public opinion nor even his own prejudices, to control him.
    William Hazlitt

Virtue can be afforded only by the poor, who have nothing to lose.
    Alexander Chase

I am a teetotaler because my family has already paid the Shaw debt to the distilling industry so magnificently as to leave me no further obligations.
    George Bernard Shaw

I would sooner have fifty unnatural vices than one unnatural virtue.
    Oscar Wilde

War

There never was a good war or a bad peace.
    Benjamin Franklin

It is not merely cruelty that leads men to love war, it is excitement.
    Henry Ward Beecher

To call war the soil of courage and virtue is like calling debauchery the soil of love.
    George Santayana

In time of war the loudest patriots are the greatest profiteers.
    August Bebel

I love war and responsibility and excitement. Peace is going to be hell on me.
    Gen. George S. Patton, Jr.

After each war there is a little less democracy to save.

> *Brooks Atkinson*

It is fatal to enter any war without the will to win it.

> *General Douglas MacArthur*

War is not healthy for children or other living things.

> *From a poster of the 1960's*

All wars are popular for the first thirty days.

> *Arthur M. Schlesinger, Jr.*

Wealth

Those who make a fortune by being miserly will not enjoy it long.

> *Chinese proverb*

Money hides many deformities.

> *Chinese proverb*

Wealth maketh many friends.

> *Proverbs 19:4*

We may see the small value God has for riches by the people he gives them to.

> *Alexander Pope*

It is better to live rich than to die rich.

> *Samuel Johnson*

I cannot understand why men should be so eager after money. Wealth is simply a superfluity of what we don't need.

> *Abraham Lincoln*

It is an unfortunate human failing that a full pocket-book often groans more loudly than an empty stomach.
>Franklin D. Roosevelt

It is only when the rich are sick that they fully feel the impotence of wealth.
>Charles Caleb Colton

It's not a sin to be rich—it's a miracle.
>W. F. Dettle

Wisdom

A wise man will learn something even from the words of a fool.
>Chinese proverb

The fear of the Lord is the beginning of wisdom.
>Psalms 111:10 and Proverbs 9:10

I don't think much of a man who is not wiser today than he was yesterday.
>Abraham Lincoln

A short man is preferable to a tall blockhead.
>Saadi

Wisdom rises upon the ruins of folly.
>Thomas Fuller

The art of being wise is the art of knowing what to overlook.
>William James

Woman

The girl who can't dance says the band can't play.
> *Yiddish proverb*

These impossible women! How they do get around us! The poet was right: can't live with them, or without them.
> *Aristophanes*

Nature has given women so much power that the law has very wisely given them little.
> *Dr. Johnson*

One must choose between loving women and knowing them.
> *Attributed to Ninon Lenclos*

Man has his will—but woman has her way.
> *Oliver Wendell Holmes, Sr.*

It is said of me that when I was young, I divided my time impartially among wine, women, and song. I deny this categorically. Ninety percent of my interests were women.
> *Arthur Rubinstein*

Women are most fascinating between the age of thirty-five and forty after they have won a few races and know how to pace themselves. Since few women ever pass forty, maximum fascination can continue indefinitely.
> *Christian Dior*

When men reach their sixties and retire, they go to pieces. Women just go right on cooking.
> *Gail Sheehy*

Work

To work is to pray.
Saint Benedict of Nursia

My father taught me to work, but not to love it. I never did like to work, and I don't deny it. I'd rather read, tell stories, crack jokes, talk, laugh—anything but work.
Abraham Lincoln

Universal idleness would speedily result in universal ruin.
Abraham Lincoln

Labor is prior to, and independent of, capital. Capital is only the fruit of labor, and could never have existed if labor had not first existed.
Abraham Lincoln

I like work; it fascinates me. I can sit and look at it for hours. I love to keep it by me; the idea of getting rid of it nearly breaks my heart.
Jerome K. Jerome

No race can prosper till it learns there is as much dignity in tilling a field as in writing a poem.
Booker T. Washington

Anyone can do any amount of work, provided it isn't the work he is supposed to be doing at the moment.
Robert C. Benchley

Work expands so as to fill time available for its completion. . . . The thing to be done swells in importance and complexity in a direct ratio with the time to be spent.
C. Northcote Parkinson

He who considers his work beneath him will be above doing it well.
Alexander Chase

World

All the world's a stage
And all the men and women merely players:
They have their exits and their entrances;
And one man in his time plays many parts,
His acts being seven ages.
William Shakespeare

The world is a comedy to those that think; a tragedy to those that feel.
Horace Walpole

The world only exists in your eyes—your conception of it. You can make it as big as or as small as you want to.
F. Scott Fitzgerald

The world has narrowed to a neighborhood before it has broadened to brotherhood.
Lyndon Baines Johnson

Youth

Every one believes in his youth that the world really began with him, and that all merely exists for his sake.
Johann Wolfgang von Goethe

In this sad world of ours, sorrow comes to all; and, to the young, it comes with bitterest agony, because it takes them unawares. The older have learned to expect it.
Abraham Lincoln

To me it seems that youth is like spring, an over-praised season—delightful if it happen to be a favoured one, but in practice very rarely favoured and more remarkable, as a general rule, for biting east winds than genial breezes. Autumn is the mellower season, and what we lose in flowers we more than gain in fruits.

Samuel Butler

I have never learned anything except from people younger than myself.

Oscar Wilde

It is better to waste one's youth than to do nothing with it at all.

Georges Courteline

Toasts

The custom of proposing toasts began thousands of years ago. Ancient warriors toasted their gods. Greeks and Romans did the same. Norsemen gave toasts to each other. In other societies—the ancient Egyptians and Chinese, for example—offering a visitor a drink and toasting a host became common courtesies.

The custom of toasting has survived countless generations since these early beginnings, and it is now firmly rooted in our own culture. So firmly rooted, in fact, that it's more than likely that sometime in your life—maybe several times—the person proposing the toast will be you. Someone may call upon you to propose a toast. Or maybe you'll just get the urge to propose one on your own. In either case, it's always nice to have something to say that captures the spirit of the moment.

The pages that follow contain a variety of toasts, all organized alphabetically according to occasion or subject matter. Thus, the first heading you'll find is *Bachelors*, and the last is *Woman*. In between are toasts that would be appropriate at graduations, wedding receptions, and on many other occasions.

If you're just having some friends over for an informal dinner, you can probably find something suitable under *Friendship. Toasts for Toasts' Sake* deals mainly in longer alternatives to such familiar toasts as *Cheers!* and *Bottoms Up!* If the occasion or the people you want to toast don't seem to fit any of the categories, try looking under *Miscellaneous*.

The "Quotations" section of this book can be another fruitful source of toasts. Many times, you can take a quotation and turn it into an appropriate toast simply by adding a few words to the beginning and the end. Here's how it would work if you were to choose one of Lincoln's quotes on friendship:

> "Ralph and I would like to tell you how very glad we are that you four special people were able to have dinner with us tonight. As Abe Lincoln once said, 'The better part of one's life consists of his friendships.' Here's to you, then, our friends."

No matter what the source of the toast itself, you need to precede it with some appropriate remark. In the example above, a quiet dinner with friends, it's enough to say that you're glad they came and that you consider them special people. At a larger, more formal occasion, you'll probably want to say a bit more. If you're attending a formal event and the chairman has just introduced you for the specific purpose of proposing a toast, you'll start by thanking him or her. Next, you'll acknowledge the presence of the others in attendance, for example, "Reverend Deems, members of the Board, ladies, and gentlemen." It's best not to try reeling off a lot of names; it takes too much time and you also run the risk of leaving someone out.

Next, you have to make reference to the reason everyone has come together. Once this is done, you're ready to honor the person or persons being toasted. You start by describing the honoree's virtues or accomplishments. Next, you express the appreciation of these virtues or accomplishments by those who have assembled for the occasion. And finally, you propose the toast. If you were doing the honors at a wedding reception, for example, your last lines might go something like this:

> "And so for all these reasons, ladies and gentlemen, I ask you to raise your glasses. [Pause here to give everyone ample opportunity to do so.] To Susan and Jerry: May their journey along the path of matrimony never meet with thorns."

Some toasters will ask those assembled to stand. In this case you would say, "Please stand and raise your glasses," allowing a little extra time for all present to get to their feet.

If you know, or even suspect, that you're going to be called upon to give a toast, it's a good idea to get some ideas in mind ahead of time. Before a very formal occasion, you should consider writing your toast out and practicing it. Use the microphone if one has been provided; if not, speak up so you can be heard at the farthest tables.

Remember that good taste never goes out of fashion. A little levity will brighten many an occasion, but if you even suspect that a joke or wisecrack might offend someone, leave it out.

Lastly, cover all the ground you have to, but keep your toast as brief as possible. A long recitation will not only bore the audience, but embarrass the honoree. Mention a few of his or her virtues and accomplishments and let it go at that.

Here's to good toasting!

Bachelors

Our future wives—Distance lends enchantment to the viewer.

Here's to our bachelors, created by God for the consolation of widows and the hope of maidens.

God made the world and rested.
God made man and rested.
Then God made woman . . .
Since then neither God nor man has had any rest.

A pipe, a book, a fire, a friend,
A stein that's always full,
Here's to the joys of a bachelor's life,
A life that is never dull.

Birthday

May you live to be a hundred years with one extra year to repent.
> *Irish proverb*

To your birthday, glass held high, Glad it's you that's older—not I.

Children

A baby will make love stronger, days shorter, nights longer, bankroll smaller, home happier, clothes shabbier, the past forgotten, and the future worth living for.

Fathers

With this toast I pay my greatest respects to the man who has so singularly honored me—by being my Father!

Here's to Dad—the kin you love to touch!

To my Dad, on his day:
"He didn't tell me how to live;
he lived,
and let me watch him do it."
Clarence Buddington Kelland

A wishful toast for all fathers—
"Father of fathers, make me one,
A fit example for a son."
Douglas Mallooch

Friendship

May the road rise to meet you. May the wind be always at your back, the sun shine warm upon your face, the rain fall soft upon your fields, and until we meet again may God hold you in the hollow of His hand.
Irish traditional

To your good health, old friend, may you live for a thousand years, and I be there to count them.
Robert Smith Surtees

Happy are we met, happy have we been,
Happy may we part, and happy meet again.

Here's to those who love us,
And here's to those who don't
A smile for those who are willing to,
And a tear for those who won't.

This glass we fill to the many gone
And the few that are left us yet.

Here's to the day of good will, cold weather and warm hearts.

Here's to Eternity—may we spend it in as good company as this night finds us.

May the friends of our youth be the companions of our old age.

If sometimes we forget a while
   That life is short and man is vile,
We do so, be it understood,
Because salvation's in a smile
   And godliness in Brotherhood.

Here's a toast to the future,
   A toast to the past,
      And a toast to our friends, far and near.
May the future be pleasant;
   The past, a bright dream;
      May our friends remain faithful and dear.

May the hinges of friendship never grow rusty.

May we have more and more friends and need them less and less.

To our friends, who know the worst about us but refuse to believe it.

Here's to you, my friend, and to friendship
For the only way to have a friend is to be one.

Old friends are scarce,
New friends are few;
Here's hoping I've found
One of each in you.

Let's not fret about the future;
  Let's not grieve about the past;
But instead, let's toast the present,
  And the friendship that will last.

May we have a few real friends rather than a thousand acquaintances.

Here's to you, my friend—may your soul be in glory long before the devil knows you're dead.

Here's to the joys of friendship,
And here's to the friend who has the bad taste to
  leave us.
May our good wishes follow him wherever he goes,
May fortune lie in wait for him,
May happiness dog his footsteps,
May success pursue and overtake him,
May he be doomed to a long life and a merry one,
And if he ever goes to a warmer place than the one
  he holds in our hearts tonight—God help him.
      Edwin L. Shuman

May we never want for a friend nor a glass to give him.

Here's to those of us who are friends and let the rest of the world make its own arrangements.

You are my friends, for you have smiled with me,
  My help and hope in fair and stormy weather;
I like you for the joys you have whiled with me,
  I love you for the griefs we've wept together.
      Nixon Waterman

May our house always be too small to hold all our friends.

Myrtle Reed

Here's to those who love us well—
Those who don't may go to Hell.

James Keene

The Future

May life be full of hope and praise,
All smiles, without a tear of sorrow;
And may our best of yesterdays
  Be bettered by our worst tomorrow.

Frank M. Morris

Here's to your future,
  Your present and your past;
May each new day
  Be happier than the last.

May the best day we have seen be worse than the worst that is to come.

Graduation

A toast to the graduate—may he always remain in a class by himself.

Here's to the sweet girl graduate—may she become even more beautiful by degrees!

Holidays

To our national birds—
  The American eagle,
  The Thanksgiving turkey:
May one give us peace in all our States—
And the other a piece for all our plates.

Eat, drink and be merry,
For tomorrow ye diet.
            Willma Gilmore Beymer

A Christmas wish—
May you never forget
what is worth remembering
or remember
what is best forgotten.

Then let us be merry and taste the good cheer,
And remember old Christmas but comes once a
    year.

Here's to the blessings of the year,
Here's to the friends we hold so dear,
To peace on earth, both far and near.

As we start the New Year,
Let's get down on our knees
to thank God we're on our feet.

Be at war with your voices, at peace with your
neighbors, and let every new year find you a better
man.
            Benjamin Franklin

Here's wishing you the kind of troubles that will last
as long as your New Year's resolutions.

In the year ahead, may we treat our friends with kindness and our enemies with generosity.

Host & Guest

May the roof above us never fall in, and may we friends gathered below never fall out.

You ask me to propose a toast
  Before these guests assembled
You wouldn't do it if you only knew
  How bad my knees have trembled.
But I'll do my best for host and guest
  By wishing one and all
A life of joy and happiness
  And may you rise from every fall.

We've had toasts to our hosts, now one to our guests, without whom it wouldn't be much of a party.

Kissing

Drink to me only with thine eyes,
  And I will pledge with mine;
Or, leave a kiss within the cup—
  I'll wash it down with wine.
        Ben Jonson

Here's to the man who kisses his sweetheart
  And kisses his sweetheart alone,
For many a man kisses another man's sweetheart
  When he thinks he's kissing his own.

To the men I've loved
To the men I've kissed
My heartfelt apologies
To the men I've missed!
118

Love & Romance

Here's a health to all them that we love,
And a health to all those that love us,
And a health to all those that love them that we
 love,
And to them that love those that love us.

Here's to one and only one,
    And may that one be he
Who loves but one and only,—
    And may that one be me.

Oh, 'tis love, 'tis love, that makes the world go
around.
        Alice's Adventures in Wonderland

Love is an ocean of emotions entirely surrounded by
expenses.
        Lord Dewar

Here's to Love that lies in Woman's eyes
And lies—and lies—and lies!

I have known many, liked a few, Loved one—Here's
to you!

Here's to those who love us,
    And here's to those who don't
A smile for those who are willing to,
    And a tear for those who won't.

Romance—the only sport in which the animal that
gets caught has to buy the license.

Here's to love—that disease which begins with a
fever and ends with a pain.

Here's to love—the only fire against which there is no insurance.

I love you
Not only for what you are,
But for what I am
When I am with you.
　　　Roy Croft

Man

Here's to the happy man: All the world loves a lover.
　　　Ralph Waldo Emerson

Here's to man—he is like a kerosene lamp; he is not especially bright; he is often turned down; he generally smokes; and he frequently goes out at night.

Men sometimes say that women suffer from vanity. But until a woman can go around with a big bald spot on the back of her head and still think she's beautiful, she can't compare with a man for vanity.

Advice to husbands—don't try to find out who is boss in the house—you'll be happier not knowing.

Marriage

Here's to marriage—a ceremony in which rings are put on the finger of the lady and through the nose of the gentleman.
　　　Herbert Spencer

Keep your eyes open before marriage—half shut afterwards.
　　　Benjamin Franklin

May those who enter the rosy paths of matrimony never meet with thorns.

The weaker sex is the stronger sex because of the weakness of the stronger sex for the weaker sex.

Matrimony—the high sea for which no compass has yet been invented.
> H. Heine

Marriage is like life in this—that it is a field of battle, and not a bed of roses.
> Robert Louis Stevenson

The battle of the sexes will never be fought to a conclusion—there is too much fraternization with the enemy.

There is only one thing for a man to do who is married to a woman who enjoys spending money, and that is to enjoy earning it.
> Edgar W. Howe

Miscellaneous

To the old, long life and treasure;
To the young, all health and pleasure.
> Ben Jonson

Old wood to burn, old wine to drink, old friends to trust, and old authors to read.
> Francis Bacon

May you live all the days of your life.
> Jonathan Swift

Here's to us all—God bless us every one.
> Charles Dickens

Let us toast the fools; but for them the rest of us
could not succeed.
        Mark Twain

Here's to all our relatives—may they forget our faults
and mend their own!

May the most you wish for be the least you get.

Here's to Home—the place where you are treated
best and grumble most.

May the sunshine of comfort dispel the clouds of despair.

May we all live in pleasure and die out of debt.

Motherhood

Here's to my dear Mother,
    For she's old and her hair is gray;
But that I love her best of all,
    I'm not ashamed to say
You may talk of your girls of beauty
    And girls of countless wealth,
But your Mother loves you best of all,
    And here's to my Mother's health.

To one whose love does last,
While lesser feelings all have passed,
I lift this toast to no one other
Than she who taught me all—my Mother!

Here's to the prettiest, the wittiest,
The truest of all who are true.
Here's to the neatest, the sweetest,
Here's to them all, Mom—here's to you!

We have toasted our sweethearts,
    Our friends and our wives,
We have toasted each other
    Wishing all merry lives;
Don't frown when I tell you
    This toast beats all others
But drink one more toast, boys—
    A toast to—Our Mothers.

Here's to Mother—may the love and appreciation of
these later days overshadow the worries we caused
her in our childhood.

Toasts for Toasts' Sake

Observe, when Mother Earth is dry
She drinks the droppings of the sky,
And then the dewy cordial gives
To every thirsty plant that lives.
The vapors which at evening weep
Are beverage to the swelling deep;
And when the rosy sun appears
He drinks the ocean's misty tears.
The moon too quaffs her paly stream
Of lusture from the solar beam.
Then hence with all your sober thinking;
Since Nature's holy law is drinking,
I'll make the law of Nature mine,
And pledge the Universe in wine.
            Tom Moore

With mirth and laughter, let old wrinkles come,
And let my liver, rather heat with wine,
Than my heart cool with mortifying gloom.
            William Shakespeare

We owe to Nature, Mother of us all,
What e'er we have of life or joy or wealth:—
Shall we not, therefore, whatsoe'er befall,
In her rich bounty pledge her gracious health?

Wedding

May those who enter the rosy paths of matrimony
never meet with thorns.
>   *Clotho*

Here's a toast to the lovely bride,
And to the husband by her side;
Here's to the home they're going to share;
May love and trust dwell with them there.

Here's to the health of the happy pair,
  May good luck meet them everywhere,
And may each day of wedded bliss
  Be always just as sweet as this!

May all single men get married
And all married men be happy.

May all your troubles be little ones.

May the warmth of our affections survive the frosts of
age.

Health, happiness and harmony to every state in the
Union—especially the married state.

Here's to my mother-in-law's daughter,
  Here's to her father-in-law's son;
And here's to the vows we've just taken,
  And the life we've just begun.

The Happy Couple—May we all live to be present at their golden wedding.

Let there be spaces in your togetherness.
    Kahlil Gibran

It is written: "When children find true love, parents find true joy." Here's to your joy and ours, from this day forward.

To the Bride and Groom—may your coming anniversaries be outnumbered only by your coming joys and pleasures!

To the Bride and Groom—may your wedding days be few and your anniversaries many.

May the joys be as deep as the ocean and their misfortunes as light as the foam.

To _____ and _____: May this be one union that will never go on strike!
    John M. Koken

Woman

Who can find a virtuous woman? for her price is far above rubies.
    Proverbs 31:10

The ladies—God bless 'em,
And may nothing distress 'em.

Here's to Woman,—The fairest work of the Great Author. The region is large, and no man should be without a copy.

Here's to our better halves,
Who reconcile us to our poorer quarters!

Here's to the woman who has a smile for every joy,
a tear for every sorrow, a consolation for every grief,
an excuse for every fault, a prayer for every misfor-
tune, and encouragement for every hope.
    Sainte-Foix

Learning is nothing without cultivated manners, but
when the two are combined in a woman you have
one of the most exquisite products of civilization.
    André Maurois